Teacher's Manual

Listen & Say It Right
in English!

Nina Weinstein

National Textbook Company
NTC a division of *NTC Publishing Group* • Lincolnwood, Illinois USA

1994 Printing

Published by National Textbook Company, a division of NTC Publishing Group.
© 1992, 1987 by NTC Publishing Group, 4255 West Touhy Avenue,
Lincolnwood (Chicago), Illinois 60646-1975 U.S.A.
Manufactured in the United States of America.

4 5 6 7 8 9 0 ML 9 8 7 6 S 9 8 7 6 5 4

CONTENTS

INTRODUCTION

Listen & Say It Right in English! enables users to improve their conversational skills and develop confidence in their abilities to speak natural, rather than textbook, English. For optimal results, students should use the accompanying audiocassettes in working with this interactive conversation/listening program. Listening skills are very important in conversation in general, and specifically in learning to choose the appropriate English register for different situations. The audiocassettes provide students with the opportunity to hear a range of voices while using the materials, and thus give them a more authentic learning experience than is possible from hearing the material from a teacher or from classmates.

This Introduction offers several suggestions that have proved effective in the classroom.

Part I

Part I of each unit is designed to introduce students to both a formal and an informal register for one particular situation. The tape will emphasize the *contrast* between formal and everyday English. Let the students listen to Part I using the tape, but stop the tape after each pair of sentences—a line in formal English and a line in everyday English. At this point, show them what the differences between the sentences are. (For example, in Unit 1, Part I, "Feeling Good," number 1— emphasize that the counterpart of the formal "Hello" is "Hi." The counterpart of the formal "How are you?" is "How's it going?") Continue in this fashion to the end of Part I.

The Practice section at the end of Part I gives students an opportunity to converse totally in one register. (For example, Unit 1, Part I, "Feeling Good," formal English, numbers 1-5.) For each unit, have them practice the formal dialogue first, then the everyday. If there are two sub-situations within a unit (as in Unit 1—"Feeling Good" and "Feeling Bad"), have students practice the first formal situation first (e.g., Unit 1, "Feeling Good," formal); then have them do the everyday counterpart ("Feeling Good," everyday). Continue until they have finished all four conversations.

Part II

In Part II, students will hear both registers of the same sentence. They will have to decide which is formal and which is everyday. This will make them sensitive to the different registers that they will actually encounter. Also, listening to the registers others are using will enable students to select the appropriate register for the right situation, rather than speaking the same way in all situations.

It's helpful again to stop the tape after each pair of sentences and perhaps do the exercise orally. Thus, if students miss the answer, you can immediately replay the sentence missed and analyze why it's the register it is. For quick reference, the tapescript for this section is provided in this Guide.

Part III

Part III moves the students further along the continuum: students were introduced to the two registers in Part I; they practiced the conversations using both registers in the Practice section; in Part II they had to decipher the difference between registers in basically the same sentence; and now, in Part III, they are given one complete formal dialogue and they must reproduce it in the everyday register.

If you assign this exercise as a written one (and the benefit to a written exercise is that it individualizes instruction—you don't have just a few students understanding and responding), have students complete it with a partner. This allows for more conversation practice.

Another way to work with this section (again in pairs) is to have students study the formal conversation and reproduce it orally (without writing) in the everyday register. Go around the room until several pairs of students have had a chance to do this.

Generally, this section is easier as a written exercise, and can thus be used with a less advanced group; practiced orally, it can be used with a more advanced group.

Part IV

Students will hear an everyday conversation *twice.* The first time, they should just listen to get the sense of the conversation. Any reduced forms that occur naturally in the conversation (e.g., *gonna, wanna,* etc.) will be heard on the tape.

After the first playing of the tape, you can stop the tape and ask various comprehension questions about the conversation. Then, continue playing the tape. The same conversation will be repeated, but there will be a short pause after each speaker's speech. Students are to fill in the blanks with the words they hear, one word for each blank. To give them additional time to write, you can either stop the tape or use the "pause" button of the tape recorder after each line. After they've finished filling in the blanks (with words or expressions learned in the current unit or in previous units), you can play the conversation once more so that they can check their answers.

For a more advanced class, you might have them fill in the blanks during the first (faster) rendition of the conversation. Remember, however, to stop the tape after each line so they have time to write. The answer key for this section is provided in this Guide.

"Other Useful Expressions," which is also on tape, gives students alternatives to some of the common expressions learned in the everyday conversation in Part IV. Make sure they understand where these expressions would naturally go in the dialogue.

Role-Play

This section gives students an opportunity to practice "Other Useful Expressions," and to transfer their new knowledge into a situation in the outside world in which they're likely to find themselves. If students want to ad lib in

Part I, let them. Make sure, however, that they don't stray from the register they're supposed to be using.

SPECIAL CULTURAL NOTES

Many of the topics presented in *Listen & Say It Right in English!* raise cultural issues that your students may be encountering for the first time. Therefore, some cultural notes are provided in the book. Of course, as you work with the units, you will want to share other cultural matters with your students. Below are a few issues that are frequently discussed.

Unit 6. Money
Note that in banks conversations are generally formal.

      Example: I'd like to open a checking account.

               savings account.

     I'd like to apply for a loan.

             credit card.

Unit 12. Lunch
Americans do not make noise when eating soup. In general, one should not make noise, or make as little noise as possible, when eating.

Unit 13. Dinner
Most foods are eaten with a fork, spoon, and/or knife. However, it is acceptable to eat fried chicken, pizza, French fries, or ribs with your fingers, unless you're in a formal restaurant. Then use a fork and knife.

When eating with guests, the host or hostess should begin eating first. Then everyone else may begin.

If you're having drinks at a restaurant, you should also tip the cocktail waitress 15% of the liquor bill.

The person who makes the drinks is called the bartender.

Unit 16. Airport
Smoking in public places (restaurants, department stores, etc.) can be very annoying to Americans. Before you smoke, be sure to ask the people around you if they mind.

     Example: Do you mind if I smoke?

Unit 19. Shopping
In many large department stores, there is a gift-wrapping service. Sometimes this service is free—especially around Christmas. You should ask the salesperson if the store has such a service, and if so, if complimentary gift-wrapping is available.

Unless you request that your purchase be gift-wrapped, the salesperson will put it in a bag.

TAPESCRIPTS — PART II
Formal or Everyday?

You will hear pairs of sentences from Part I. One will be a formal sentence and one will be an everyday sentence. As you listen, write "formal" if you hear a formal sentence; write "everyday" if you hear an everyday sentence.

UNIT ONE

1.   Hello. How are you?
2.   Hi. How's it going?

1.   formal
2.   everyday

3.   Great.
4.   Fine, thanks.

3.   everyday
4.   formal

5.   Oh? That's too bad.
6.   Oh? I'm sorry to hear that.

5.   everyday
6.   formal

7.   It was nice to see you.
8.   It was great seeing you.

7.   formal
8.   everyday

9.   Hi. How's it going?
10.   Hello. How are you?

9.   everyday
10.   formal

11.   Well, I'll be just like new in no time.
12.   Well, I'm sure I'll recover soon.

11.   everyday
12.   formal

13.   Fine, thank you. And you?
14.   Not bad. How about you?

13.   formal
14.   everyday

15. Take it easy, and I hope you get better soon.
16. Take care of yourself, and I hope you feel better soon.

15. everyday
16. formal

17. Oh no. I have to be going. I have a meeting at ten.
18. Uh oh. I've got to get moving. I've got a meeting at ten.

17. formal
18. everyday

19. I'm not doing very well. I have a cold.
20. Not so good. I've got a cold.

19. formal
20. everyday

UNIT TWO

1. Beautiful weather we're having, isn't it?
2. Great weather, isn't it?

1. formal
2. everyday

3. Fifth, please.
4. Fifth, please.

3. formal or everyday
4. formal or everyday

5. Things are a little slow now, but I'm sure they'll pick up soon. Say hello to your family for me.
6. Things are a little slow now, but I'm sure we'll be busy again soon. Give my regards to your family.

5. everyday
6. formal

7. Oh, it's very busy. What about you?
8. Oh, it's really crazy. How about you?

7. formal
8. everyday

9. Yeah, I really love hot weather.
10. Yes, I enjoy hot weather.

9. everyday
10. formal

11. What floor?
12. What floor would you like?

11.   everyday
12.   formal

13.   Great. Just great. And you?
14.   Fine. Just fine. And you?

13.   everyday
14.   formal

15.   Well, have a nice day.
16.   Well, have a good day.

15.   formal
16.   everyday

17.   Great. How's work?
18.   Fine. How is work going?

17.   everyday
18.   formal

19.   Hi, Fred. How are you doing?
20.   Hello, Fred. How are you?

19.   everyday
20.   formal

UNIT THREE

1.   How do you do?
2.   How are you?

1.   formal
2.   everyday

3.   We play golf together. And you?
4.   We play golf together. How about you?

3.   formal
4.   everyday

5.   I'm a businessman. What do you do?
6.   I'm a businessman. What kind of work do you do?

5.   everyday
6.   formal

7.   Hello. I'm Tim Johnson.
8.   Hi. I'm Tim Johnson.

7.   formal
8.   everyday

9.   I think your chances are really good. Here's my card.
     Give me a call when you graduate and I'll see what I can
     do.
10. I think the opportunities are very good. Here's my card.
     Why don't you give me a call when you graduate and I'll
     see what I can do for you.

9.   everyday
10. formal

11. We met in college. What do you do for a living?
12. We met in college. What kind of work do you do?

11. everyday
12. formal

13. Hello. What do you plan to do when you complete
     college?
14. Hi. What do you plan to do when you finish college?

13. formal
14. everyday

15. How do you do?
16. How are you?

15. formal
16. everyday

17. Juan Valdez, this is Carlos Ramirez. Carlos works for a
     computer company. Carlos, this is Juan. Juan is studying
     computers in college.
18. Juan, this is Carlos. Carlos works for a computer
     company. Carlos, Juan. Juan's studying computers in col-
     lege.

17. formal
18. everyday

19. Become a computer programmer. What do you think my
     chances are in that field?
20. I'd like to become a computer programmer. What do you
     think about the opportunities in that field?

19. everyday
20. formal

UNIT FOUR

1.   Have you had a chance to look over my report yet?
2.   Have you had an opportunity to look over my report yet?

1. everyday
2. formal

3. What a beautiful house!
4. What a beautiful house!

3. formal or everyday
4. formal or everyday

5. Thank you. We recently redecorated.
6. Thanks. We just redecorated.

5. formal
6. everyday

7. What do you think?
8. What do you think?

7. formal or everyday
8. formal or everyday

9. You did a super job. The sales figures were really helpful.
10. I think you did a wonderful job. The sales figures you included were especially helpful.

9. everyday
10. formal

11. It's dynamite.
12. It's gorgeous.

11. everyday
12. formal

13. Yes, as a matter fact, I did.
14. Uh huh. As a matter fact, I did.

13. formal
14. everyday

15. Do you want to see our new patio?
16. Would you like to see our new patio?

15. everyday
16. formal

17. I'd love to.
18. Sure.

17. formal
18. everyday

19. Thank you very much.
20. Thanks.

19.   formal
20.   everyday

UNIT FIVE

1.   What did you think of the movie?
2.   How did you like the movie?

1.   formal
2.   everyday

3.   Oh, it was okay.
4.   Well, it was nothing special.

3.   everyday
4.   formal

5.   Me too.
6.   I agree.

5.   everyday
6.   formal

7.   What didn't you like?
8.   What was your criticism?

7.   everyday
8.   formal

9.   It was difficult for me to imagine John Wayne as a businessman. That ruined the movie for me.
10.   It was hard to imagine John Wayne as a businessman. That destroyed the movie for me.

9.   formal
10.   everyday

11.   I thought the ending was the pits. I hate sad endings.
12.   I thought the ending was terrible. I don't like sad endings.

11.   everyday
12.   formal

13.   That's a good point, but I think John Wayne did a good job. I think it was the script that was bad.
14.   That's a good point, but I think John Wayne did a good job. It was the script that was lousy.

13.   formal
14.   everyday

15.   How did you like the movie?
16.   What did you think of the movie?

15.   everyday
16.   formal

17.   Well, it was nothing special.
18.   Oh, it was okay.

17.   formal
18.   everyday

19.   What was your criticism?
20.   What didn't you like?

19.   formal
20.   everyday

UNIT SIX

1.   Cash or charge?
2.   Will that be cash or charge?

1.   everyday
2.   formal

3.   Check.
4.   Check.

3.   formal or everyday
4.   formal or everyday

5.   I don't have two forms of identification. Will you accept a fifty-dollar traveler's check?
6.   I haven't got two ID's. How about a fifty-dollar traveler's check?

5.   formal
6.   everyday

7.   Excuse me. How much is this wallet?
8.   Pardon me. How much is this wallet?

7.   everyday
8.   formal

9.   It's $25.99 plus tax.
10. $25.99 plus tax.

9.   formal
10.   everyday

11. Okay. That comes to $27.55. Out of $50? $27.65, $.75, $28, $29, $30, $40, and $50. Thank you and come again.
12. Fine. That comes to $27.55. Out of $50? $27.65, $.75, $28, $29, $30, $40, and $50. Thank you very much and come again.

11. everyday
12. formal

13. Then I'll need to see two forms of identification—a driver's license and a major credit card.
14. Then I'll have to have two ID's—a driver's license and a major credit card.

13. formal
14. everyday

15. Is it genuine leather?
16. Is it real leather?

15. formal
16. everyday

17. Yes.
18. Yes, it is.

17. everyday
18. formal

19. Okay. I'll take it.
20. All right. I'll take it.

19. everyday.
20. formal.

UNIT SEVEN

1. Mr. Schwartz is on another line. Would you care to hold?
2. Bob's on another line. Can you hold?

1. formal
2. everyday

3. Hunter Business Machines. Can I help you?
4. Hunter Business Machines. May I help you?

3. everyday
4. formal

5. Sure. Thank you.
6. Yes, thank you.

5. everyday
6. formal

7. Yes. I'd like to speak to Bob Schwartz. This is Tina
   Williams calling.
8. Yes. Bob Schwartz, please. This is Tina Williams.

7. formal
8. everyday

9. Mr. Schwartz? How are you?
10. Bob? How are you doing?

9. formal
10. everyday

UNIT EIGHT

1. Can I help you?
2. What can I do for you?

1. everyday
2. formal

3. Yes, please.
4. Yes, please.

3. formal or everyday
4. formal or everyday

5. Sure. Would you like me to check under the hood?
6. You bet. Do you want me to check under the hood?

5. formal
6. everyday

7. Can I have a quart of Pennzoil 10/40?
8. May I have a quart of Pennzoil 10/40?

7. everyday
8. formal

9. Sure. Do you want your windows washed?
10. Sure. Would you like me to wash your windows?

9. everyday
10. formal

11. Yes, please.
12. Yeah, please.

11. formal
12. everyday

13. Would you please give me ten dollars' worth of regular unleaded?
14. Could you please give me ten dollars' worth of regular unleaded?

13. formal
14. everyday

15. You're a quart low on oil.
16. You're a quart low on oil.

15. formal or everyday
16. formal or everyday

17. That'll be $11.75. Out of $20? $11.75, $12, $13, $14, $15, and $20. Thanks and come again.
18. That comes to $11.75. Out of $20? $11.75, $12, $13, $14, $15, and $20. Thank you very much and come again.

17. everyday
18. formal

19. Thank you.
20. Thank you.

19. formal or everyday
20. formal or everyday

UNIT NINE

1. Excuse me. Could you tell me where Wilshire Boulevard is? We're lost.
2. Excuse me. Where's Wilshire Boulevard? We're lost.

1. formal
2. everyday

3. Pardon me. Could you tell me where Room 240 is?
4. Excuse me. Can you tell me where Room 240 is?

3. formal
4. everyday

5. Thanks a lot.
6. Thank you very much.

7. Uh huh.
8. Your're welcome.

7. everyday
8. formal

9.   Take the elevator to the second floor and turn right.
10.   Take the elevator to the second floor and turn right.

9.   formal or everyday
10.   formal or everyday

11.   We're lost. There's a gas station. Why don't we drive in
      and ask for directions?
12.   We're lost. There's a gas station. Let's pull in and get
      directions.

11.   formal
12.   everyday

13.   All right. Turn left out of the driveway over there. Then
      go straight for about a mile. You'll cross Santa Monica
      Boulevard. Right after that, you'll see Wilshire.
14.   Okay. Turn left out of the driveway over there. Then go
      straight for a mile or so. You'll cross Santa Monica
      Boulevard. Right after that, you'll see Wilshire.

13.   formal
14.   everyday

15.   Sure. Go to the end of this hallway and turn left. You'll
      see an elevator.
16.   All right. Go to the end of this hallway and turn left.
      You'll see an elevator.

15.   everyday
16.   formal

17.   Uh huh.
18.   Yes.

17.   everyday
18.   formal

19.   Thanks a lot.
20.   Thank you very much.

19.   everyday
20.   formal

UNIT TEN

1.   I'm starving. How about you?
2.   I'm famished. Are you hungry?

1.   everyday
2.   formal

3. Yeah, but it's my treat this time.
4. Yes, but I'd like to take you this time.

3. everyday
4. formal

5. I'd like to, but I can't this time. Can we make it another time?
6. I want to, but I can't. Can we take a rain check?

5. formal
6. everyday

7. Sure.
8. Yes, of course.

7. everyday
8. formal

9. No. I invited you.
10. Nope. I asked you.

9. formal
10. everyday

11. Yes, I'm very hungry.
12. Yeah. I'm so hungry I could eat a cow.

11. formal
12. everyday

13. I hear there's a good Japanese restaurant near here. Would you like to go there for lunch?
14. I hear there's a good Japanese restaurant close by. Do you want to go there for lunch?

13. formal
14. everyday

15. I hear there's a good Japanese restaurant close by. Do you want to go there for lunch?
16. I hear there's a good Japanese restaurant near here. Would you like to go there for lunch?

15. everyday
16. formal

17. I'm famished. Are you hungry?
18. I'm starving. How about you?

17. formal
18. everyday

19.   Oh, I'm a little bit hungry.
20.   Oh, I'm a little hungry.

19.   everyday
20.   formal

UNIT ELEVEN

1.   Are you ready to order?
2.   Ready to order?

1.   formal
2.   everyday

3.   Yes. I'd like the bacon and eggs breakfast.
4.   Yeah. I want the bacon and eggs breakfast.

3.   formal
4.   everyday

5.   What kind of toast would you like?
6.   What kind of toast?

5.   formal
6.   everyday

7.   Do you want coffee to start?
8.   Would you like coffee to start?

7.   everyday
8.   formal

9.   Yes, please.
10.   Please.

9.   formal
10.   everyday

11.   White, wheat, rye, sour dough, or English muffins.
12.   White, wheat, rye, sour dough, or English muffins.

11.   formal or everyday
12.   formal or everyday

13.   What have you got?
14.   What do you have?

13.   everyday
14.   formal

15.   How do you want your eggs?
16.   How would you like your eggs?

15. everyday
16. formal

17. Over easy.
18. Over easy.

17. formal or everyday
18. formal or everyday

19. I'll have an English muffin, please.
20. An English muffin, please.

19. formal
20. everyday

UNIT TWELVE

1. Anything else I can get you?
2. Is there anything else I can get for you?

1. everyday
2. formal

3. No, thank you. Just the check, please.
4. No, thanks. Just the check.

3. formal
4. everyday

5. Okay. Thank you.
6. All right. Thank you very much.

5. everyday
6. formal

7. Would you care for anything to drink?
8. Anything to drink?

7. formal
8. everyday

9. I'll have a glass of milk, please.
10. A glass of milk, please.

9. formal
10. everyday

11. Large or small?
12. Would you like a large or small glass of milk?

11. everyday
12. formal

13.   A small one will be fine.
14.   Small, please.

13.   formal
14.   everyday

15.   Thank you.
16.   Thank you.

15.   formal or everyday
16.   formal or everyday

17.   Ready to order?
18.   Are you ready to order?

17.   everyday
18.   formal

19.   Yes. I want a roast beef on rye.
20.   Yes. I'd like a roast beef sandwich on rye bread.

19.   everyday
20.   formal

UNIT THIRTEEN

1.   Would you like a cocktail?
2.   Can I get you a drink?

1.   formal
2.   everyday

3.   Please. I think I'll have a Bloody Mary.
4.   Yes, please. I think I'd like a Bloody Mary.

3.   everyday
4.   formal

5.   How do you want your steak?
6.   How would you like your steak?

5.   everyday
6.   formal

7.   Medium, please. A baked potato with sour cream and chives. And salad with French dressing.
8.   Medium, please. A baked potato with sour cream and chives. And salad with French dressing.

7.   formal or everyday
8.   formal or everyday

9.   Are you ready to order?
10.   Are you ready to order?

9. formal or everyday
10. formal or everyday

11. No. I'd like a few more minutes, please.
12. Not quite. I need a few more minutes.

11. formal
12. everyday

13. What can I get you?
14. What would you like?

13. everyday
14. formal

15. The steak dinner.
16. I'd like the steak dinner.

15. everyday
16. formal

17. Fine. I'll be back in a few minutes.
18. Okay. I'll come back in a few minutes.

17. formal
18. everyday

19. Thank you very much.
20. Thank you.

19. formal
20. everyday

UNIT FOURTEEN

1. How about an after-dinner drink?
2. How about an after-dinner drink?

1. formal or everyday
2. formal or everyday

3. That sounds great.
4. That sounds nice.

3. everyday
4. formal

5. How's your steak?
6. How is your steak?

5. everyday
6. formal

7.   Delicious. How is yours?
8.   Super. How's yours?

7.   formal
8.   everyday

9.   Wonderful. Would you pass the salt, please?
10.   Great. Could you pass the salt, please?

9.   formal
10.   everyday

11.   Well, ready to go?
12.   Well, are you ready to leave?

11.   everyday
12.   formal

13.   Yes. Thank you very much for the lovely dinner.
14.   Yeah. Thanks so much for the great dinner.

13.   formal
14.   everyday

15.   It was my pleasure. We'll have to do it again sometime.
16.   I enjoyed it too. Let's do it again sometime.

15.   formal
16.   everyday

17.   Uh huh. How about some dessert?
18.   Here you are. Would you like some dessert?

17.   everyday
18.   formal

19.   Oh, no thank you. I'm completely full.
20.   Oh, no thanks. I'm stuffed.

19.   formal
20.   everyday

UNIT FIFTEEN

1.   I purchased this tape recorder here last week and now it
      doesn't seem to be working.
2.   I bought this tape recorder here last week and now it
      doesn't work.

1.   formal
2.   everyday

3. You're right. There's something wrong. Do you want a refund, or do you want to exchange it?
4. You're right. There's something wrong with it. Would you like a refund, or do you want to exchange it?

3. everyday
4. formal

5. I'd like to exchange it, please.
6. I want to exchange it, please.

5. formal
6. everyday

7. Pardon me. I ordered a medium steak and this one seems to be rare.
8. Excuse me. I ordered a medium steak and this one is rare.

7. formal
8. everyday

9. Oh, really?
10. Oh?

9. formal
10. everyday

11. Hmmm. Let me see.
12. Oh? May I take a look?

11. everyday
12. formal

13. Could you take it back to the kitchen?
14. I'd like to send it back to the kitchen.

13. everyday
14. formal

15. I brought my receipt.
16. I've got my receipt.

15. formal
16. everyday

17. Sure. Sorry for the mix-up.
18. Certainly. I'm sorry for the mistake.

17. everyday
18. formal

19. No problem.
20. That's all right.

19. everyday
20. formal

UNIT SIXTEEN

1. May I help you?
2. May I help you?

1. formal or everyday
2. formal or everyday

3. Yes. I want to make a round-trip reservation from Los Angeles to New York on Tuesday, June 23.
4. Yes. I'd like to make a round-trip reservation from Los Angeles to New York on Tuesday, June 23.

3. everyday
4. formal

5. We've got a 10:00 p.m. return.
6. We have a 10:00 p.m. return flight.

5. everyday
6. formal

7. Fine.
8. Great.

7. formal
8. everyday

9. Okay. What time do you want to leave L.A.?
10. All right. What time would you like to leave Los Angeles?

9. everyday
10. formal

11. All right. I have you booked on Flight 64 departing Los Angeles on June 23 at 3:10 p.m.
12. Okay. I've got you down for Flight 63 leaving L.A. on June 23 at 3:10 p.m.

11. formal
12. everyday

13. That will be fine. I'd like a return flight on June 26. In the late evening.
14. That'll be fine. I want to come back on June 26. Late evening.

13. formal
14. everyday

15. Do you have any flights around 3 p.m.?
16. Have you got any flights around 3 p.m.?

15. formal
16. everyday

17. Yes. There's a flight departing at 3:10.
18. Yes. There's a flight leaving at 3:10.

17. formal
18. everyday

19. Non-smoking, please.
20. Non-smoking, please.

19. formal or everyday
20. formal or everyday

UNIT SEVENTEEN

1. All right. Is that your luggage over there?
2. Sure. Are those your bags over there?

1. formal
2. everyday

3. Taxi! Taxi!
4. Taxi! Taxi!

3. formal or everyday
4. formal or everyday

5. Would you please send a taxi to 9725 Wilshire Boulevard in Beverly Hills?
6. Could you please send a taxi to 9725 Wilshire Boulevard in Beverly Hills?

5. formal
6. everyday

7. Oh, around $15.00.
8. Oh, it'll be about $15.00

7. everyday
8. formal

9. Okay. When do you want it?
10. All right. When would you like it?

9. everyday
10. formal

11. Right away.
12. As soon as possible.

11.   everyday
12.   formal

13.   We want to go to the Bonaventure Hotel.
14.   We'd like to go to the Bonaventure Hotel.

13.   everyday
14.   formal

15.   Okay. There'll be a cab there in about twenty minutes.
16.   All right. There will be a taxi there within twenty minutes.

15.   everyday
16.   formal

17.   Yeah. Thanks. About how much is the fare?
18.   Yes. Thank you. Approximately how much is the fare?

17.   everyday
18.   formal

19.   Thank you.
20.   Thanks.

19.   formal
20.   everyday

UNIT EIGHTEEN

1.   Could you spell the last name?
2.   Would you spell the last name, please?

1.   everyday
2.   formal

3.   Yes. N-I-S-H-I-M-O-T-O.
4.   Uh huh. N-I-S-H-I-M-O-T-O.

3.   formal
4.   everyday

5.   Right over there, please.
6.   Over there, please.

5.   formal
6.   everyday

7.   Hello. I have a reservation for 6 p.m.
      Haruo Nishimoto.
8.   Hi. I've got a reservation for 6 p.m.
      Haruo Nishimoto.

7.   formal
8.   everyday

9.   Yes. Is there anything I can get for you?
10.   Uh huh. Anything I can get you?

9.   formal
10.   everyday

11.   No, thanks.
12.   No, I'm fine, thank you.

11.   formal
12.   everyday

13.   Yes. I have your reservation right here. Would you please complete this registration form?
14.   Yes. Here we are. Please fill out this registration form.

13.   formal
14.   everyday

15.   Well, if you need anything, just call the bell captain. The number is on the phone.
16.   Well, if you need anything, please call the bell captain. The number is on the telephone.

15.   everyday
16.   formal

17.   Is there Room Service twenty-four hours?
18.   Is Room Service available twenty-four hours?

17.   everyday
18.   formal

19.   Certainly.
20.   Sure.

19.   formal
20.   everyday

UNIT NINETEEN

1.   May I help you?
2.   Can I help you?

1.   formal
2.   everyday

3.   No, thanks. I'm just looking around.
4.   No, thank you. I'm just browsing.

3.   everyday
4.   formal

5.   Pardon me. Could you tell me where the milk is?
6.   Excuse me. Where's the milk?

5.   formal
6.   everyday

7.   Down aisle 12 in the dairy section.
8.   It's down aisle 12 in the dairy section.

7.   everyday
8.   formal

9.   In the corner of the store, in the produce section. And
        when you're through, the check-out stand is over there.
10.   It's in the corner of the market, in the produce section.
        And when you finish, the check-out stand is over there.

9.   everyday
10.   formal

11.   Thanks a lot.
12.   Thank you very much.

11.   everyday
12.   formal

13.   All right. What size shirt do you wear?
14.   Okay. What size?

13.   formal
14.   everyday

15.   Well, if you find anything you're interested in, I'll be
        happy to help you.
16.   Okay. If you find anything you like, just let me know.

15.   formal
16.   everyday

17.   Now that you mention it, I do want a shirt.
18.   Now that you mention it, I do want a shirt.

17.   formal or everyday
18.   formal or everyday

19.   Thank you. And where is the fruit?
20.   Thanks. Uh, where's the fruit?

19.   formal
20.   everyday

UNIT TWENTY

1. Do you have a quarter I could borrow? I've got to make a call and I don't have change.
2. I wonder if I could trouble you for a quarter. I have to make a telephone call and I don't have any change.

1. everyday
2. formal

3. Thanks a lot. You were a big help.
4. Thank you for your time. You were very helpful.

3. everyday
4. formal

5. Could you check these papers? I'm not sure I did them right.
6. Would you mind looking over these papers? I'm not sure I did them correctly.

5. everyday
6. formal

7. No. Sorry.
8. I'm sorry, but I don't.

7. everyday
8. formal

9. Well, thank you for the quarter. I'll return it as soon as I get change.
10. Well, thanks for the quarter. I'll pay it back as soon as I get some change.

9. formal
10. everyday

11. I'd be happy to. What specifically would you like me to check?
12. Sure. Anything in particular you want me to check?

11. formal
12. everyday

13. I hate to bother you again, but do you happen to know the number of the Del Amo Theater?
14. By the way, do you know the number of the Del Amo Theater?

13. formal
14. everyday

15.   Uh, the charts were a real problem.
16.   Well, I found the charts very difficult.

15.   everyday
16.   formal

17.   They look fine to me.
18.   They look great to me.

17.   formal
18.   everyday

19.   Sure thing.
20.   Certainly.

19.   everyday
20.   formal

UNIT TWENTY-ONE

1.   What are your symptoms?
2.   What are your symptoms?

1.   formal or everyday
2.   formal or everyday

3.   Well, I've got a fever, chills, and nausea.
4.   Well, I have a fever, chills, and nausea.

3.   everyday
4.   formal

5.   Oh no! I've lost my wallet!
6.   Uh oh! My wallet's gone.

5.   formal
6.   everyday

7.   Let's report it to the police.
8.   I think we should report it to the police.

7.   everyday
8.   formal

9.   Let's retrace your steps. Where did you last have it?
10.   Why don't we retrace your steps? Where did you last have it?

9.   everyday
10.   formal

11.   On the bus. Oh no! I think someone stole it!
12.   On the bus. Uh oh! Someone lifted it!

11. formal
12. everyday

13. Some steak, a lobster, soup, salad, a few cocktails, potatoes, chocolate pie...
14. Some steak, a lobster, soup, salad, a couple of drinks, potatoes, chocolate pie...

13. formal
14. everyday

15. Have you eaten anything unusual in the last twenty-four hours?
16. Have you had anything you're not used to in the last twenty-four hours?

15. formal
16. everyday

17. My stomach is upset.
18. My stomach is killing me.

17. formal
18. everyday

19. All right. I'll have to call the bank and inform them as well.
20. Okay. I've got to call the bank and tell them too.

19. formal
20. everyday

UNIT TWENTY-TWO

1. My pleasure. Say hi to your family for me.
2. It was my pleasure. Please give my regards to your family.

1. everyday
2. formal

3. I really think we have to increase productivity...
4. I strongly feel we need to increase productivity...

3. everyday
4. formal

5. I'm so glad you could make it. I had a great time.
6. I'm so glad you could come. I had a wonderful time.

5. everyday
6. formal

7.   Well, you've said some interesting things, but I have to think it over.
8.   Well, you've made some interesting points, but I'd like some time to think about what you've said.

7.   everyday
8.   formal

9.   When will you get back to me?
10.   When do you think you'll have a decision?

9.   everyday
10.   formal

11.   Me too. Thanks for asking me here.
12.   So did I. Thank you for inviting me here.

11.   everyday
12.   formal

13.   Why don't you give me a few days? Thank you very much for your time. It was very informative.
14.   In a few days. Thank you for your time. It was very informative.

13.   formal
14.   everyday

15.   You bet.
16.   You're welcome.

15.   everyday
16.   formal

17.   Well, I'd better get going. I've got to get up at the crack of dawn tomorrow.
18.   Well, I'd better be leaving. I have to get up very early tomorrow.

17.   everyday
18.   formal

19.   And give my regards to yours.
20.   You too.

19.   formal
20.   everyday

ANSWER KEY—PART IV

UNIT 1. GREETINGS

1. How's 2. going 3. How 4. about 5. you 6. Not 7. so
8. That's 9. too 10. bad 11. just 12. like 13. new 14. no 15. time
16. take 17. it 18. easy 19. got 20. to 21. get 22. moving 23. great
24. seeing 25. Great 26. seeing 27. you

UNIT 2. SMALL TALK

1. How 2. are 3. you 4. doing 5. Great 6. How 7. about 8. you 9. Just
10. great 11. please 12. how's 13. work 14. really 15. crazy 16. How
17. about 18. you 19. How's 20. it 21. going 22. things 23. are 24. a
25. little 26. slow 27. they'll 28. pick 29. up 30. say 31. hello 32. to
33. your 34. family

UNIT 3. MORE SMALL TALK

1. Hi 2. I'm 3. Nice 4. to 5. meet 6. you 7. I'm 8. Nice 9. to 10. meet
11. you 12. Great 13. What 14. do 15. you 16. do 17. How 18. about
19. you 20. I'm 21. a 22. does 23. he 24. Nice 25. to 26. meet 27. you
28. Nice 29. to 30. meet 31. you

UNIT 4. GIVING A COMPLIMENT

1. What 2. a 3. Beautiful 4. house 5. Thanks 6. dynamite 7. Do 8. you
9. want 10. to 11. see 12. You 13. did 14. a 15. super 16. job
17. really 18. loved

UNIT 5. CRITICIZING AND DISAGREEING

1. How 2. did 3. you 4. like 5. the 6. pits 7. What 8. didn't 9. you
10. like 11. was 12. lousy 13. destroyed 14. That's 15. a 16. good
17. point 18. but 19. I 20. think 21. really 22. love

UNIT 6. MONEY

1. Excuse 2. me 3. How 4. much 5. is 6. this 7. Is 8. it 9. real
10. leather 11. I'll 12. take 13. it 14. Cash 15. or 16. charge 17. Check
18. I'll 19. have 20. to 21. have 22. a 23. driver's 24. license 25. and
26. a 27. major 28. credit 29. card 30. I 31. haven't 32. got 33. a
34. credit 35. card 36. That 37. comes 38. to 39. Thank 40. you 41. and
42. come 43. again 44. Thank 45. you

UNIT 7. TELEPHONE

1. Can 2. I 3. help 4. you 5. on 6. another 7. line 8. Can 9. you
10. hold 11. line 12. How 13. are 14. you 15. doing 16. And 17. you
18. Great

UNIT 8. FILLING IT UP

1. Could 2. you 3. please 4. give 5. me 6. worth 7. of 8. regular
9. unleaded 10. You 11. bet 12. want 13. me 14. to 15. check 16. under
17. the 18. hood 19. You're 20. two 21. quarts 22. low 23. on 24. oil
25. Can 26. I 27. have 28. two 29. quarts 30. of 31. Sure 32. Do 33. you
34. want 35. your 36. windows 37. washed 38. That'll 39. be 40. checks
41. Credit 42. cards 43. I've 44. got

UNIT 9. GETTING DIRECTIONS

1. We're 2. lost 3. Let's 4. pull 5. into 6. a 7. gas 8. station 9. and
10. get 11. directions 12. Excuse 13. me 14. Where's 15. We're 16. lost
17. Turn 18. left 19. out 20. of 21. the 22. driveway 23. go 24. straight
25. for 26. a 27. mile 28. or 29. so 30. on 31. your 32. left 33. go 34. to
35. the 36. end 37. of 38. the 39. hallway 40. to 41. the 42. second
43. floor 44. and 45. turn 46. right 47. Thanks 48. a 49. lot 50. Sure
51. turn 52. right 53. out 54. of 55. the 56. driveway

UNIT 10. INVITING SOMEONE OUT

1. I'm 2. so 3. hungry 4. I 5. could 6. eat 7. a 8. cow 9. How 10. about
11. you 12. close 13. by 14. Do 15. you 16. want 17. to 18. go 19. there
20. for 21. lunch 22. I 23. want 24. to 25. but 26. I 27. can't 28. that's
29. too 30. bad 31. rain 32. check 33. Sure 34. Great 35. my 36. treat
37. Nope 38. I 39. asked 40. you

UNIT 11. BREAKFAST

1. Do 2. you 3. want 4. coffee 5. to 6. start 7. Please 8. Yeah 9. Ready
10. to 11. order 12. I 13. want 14. the 15. sausage 16. and 17. eggs
18. How 19. do 20. you 21. want 22. your 23. eggs 24. What 25. kind
26. of 27. toast 28. What 29. have 30. you 31. got 32. Wheat 33. Thank
34. you 35. and 36. come 37. again

UNIT 12. LUNCH

1. Ready 2. to 3. order 4. I 5. want 6. a 7. ham 8. on 9. rye
10. anything 11. to 12. drink 13. a 14. glass 15. of 16. mile 17. Large
18. or 19. small 20. Anything 21. else 22. I 23. can 24. get 25. you
26. No 27. thanks 28. Just 29. the 30. check

UNIT 13. DINNER

1. Can 2. I 3. get 4. you 5. a 6. drink 7. I 8. think 9. I'll 10. have
11. a 12. Scotch 13. on 14. the 15. rocks 16. Are 17. you 18. ready
19. to 20. order 21. Not 22. quite 23. What 24. can 25. I 26. get 27. you
28. how 29. do 30. you 31. want 32. your 33. steak 34. Baked 35. please
36. With 37. sour 38. cream 39. and 40. chives

UNIT 14. CONVERSATION DURING A MEAL

1. Great 2. How's 3. your 4. steak 5. Super 6. Could 7. you 8. please
9. pass 10. the 11. salt 12. how 13. about 14. some 15. dessert 16. I'm
17. stuffed 18. An 19. after 20. dinner 21. drink 22. That 23. sounds
24. great 25. ready 26. to 27. go 28. Thanks 29. so 30. much 31. for
32. the 33. great 34. dinner 35. I 36. enjoyed 37. it 38. too 39. Let's
40. do 41. it 42. again 43. sometime

UNIT 15. COMPLAINING ABOUT SERVICE

1. excuse 2. me 3. I 4. bought 5. this 6. and 7. now 8. it 9. doesn't
10. work 11. Let 12. me 13. see 14. I've 15. got 16. my 17. receipt
18. There's 19. something 20. wrong 21. Do 22. you 23. want 24. a
25. refund 26. or 27. do 28. you 29. want 30. to 31. exchange 32. it
33. I 34. want 35. to 36. exchange 37. it 38. please

UNIT 16. AIRPORT

1. May 2. I 3. help 4. you 5. I 6. want 7. to 8. make 9. a 10. round
11. trip 12. reservation 13. from 14. to 15. When 16. do 17. you 18. want
19. to 20. leave 21. a 22. flight 23. leaving 24. and 25. arriving 26. Late
27. evening 28. We've 29. got 30. a 31. return 32. flight 33. I've 34. got
35. you 36. down 37. for 38. leaving 39. and 40. arriving 41. Your
42. return 43. flight 44. is 45. leaving 46. and 47. arriving 48. Do 49. you
50. want 51. a 52. smoking 53. or 54. non-smoking 55. section

UNIT 17. TAXI

1. We 2. want 3. to 4. go 5. to 6. the 7. Are 8. those 9. your 10. bags
11. over 12. there 13. About 14. how 15. much 16. is 17. the 18. fare
19. around 20. thanks 21. a 22. lot 23. bags

UNIT 18. HOTEL

1. I've 2. got 3. a 4. reservation 5. for 6. Could 7. you 8. spell 9. the
10. last 11. name 12. please 13. Sure 14. Please 15. fill 16. out 17. this
18. registration 19. form 20. Anything 21. I 22. can 23. get 24. you

UNIT 19. SHOPPING

1. Can 2. I 3. help 4. you 5. I'm 6. just 7. looking 8. around
10. like 11. just 12. let 13. me 14. know 15. What 16. size 17. Do
18. you 19. want 20. to 21. how 22. do 23. they 24. How 25. about
26. How 27. about

UNIT 20. ASKING A FAVOR

1. Excuse 2. me 3. Do 4. you 5. have 6. I 7. hate 8. to 9. bother
10. you 11. but 12. do 13. you 14. happen 15. to 16. have 17. a 18. real
19. problem 20. Could 21. you 22. help 23. me 24. No 25. problem
26. You 27. were 28. a 29. big 30. help

UNIT 21. TROUBLE, TROUBLE, TROUBLE

1. killing 2. me 3. What 4. are 5. your 6. symptoms 7. nausea 8. fever
9. Let's 10. fever 11. and 12. nausea 13. lifted 14. to 15. treat 16. Did
17. you 18. have 19. you're 20. not 21. used 22. to 23. couple 24. of
25. drinks

UNIT 22. GOODBYE

1. really 2. think 3. very 4. interesting 5. conversation 6. but 7. I've
8. got 9. to 10. get 11. up 12. at 13. the 14. crack 15. of 16. dawn
17. I'm 18. so 19. glad 20. you 21. could 22. make 23. it 24. I 25. had
26. a 27. great 28. time 29. Thanks 30. for 31. asking 32. me 33. My
34. pleasure 35. to 36. say 37. hi 38. to 39. your 40. family 41. for 42. me

NTC ESL/EFL TEXTS AND MATERIAL
Junior High—Adult Education

Computer Software
Amigo
Basic Vocabulary Builder on Computer

Language and Culture Readers
Beginner's English Reader
Advanced Beginner's English Reader
Cultural Encounters in the U.S.A.
Passport to America Series
  California Discovery
  Adventures in the Southwest
  The Coast-to-Coast Mystery
  The New York Connection
Discover America Series
  California, Chicago, Florida, Hawaii,
  New England, New York, Texas,
  Washington, D.C.
Looking at America Series
  Looking at American Signs, Looking at
  American Food, Looking at American
  Recreation, Looking at American Holidays
Time: We the People
Communicative American English
English á la Cartoon

Text/Audiocassette Learning Packages
Speak Up! Sing Out!
Listen and Say It Right in English!

Transparencies
Everyday Situations in English

Duplicating Masters and
Black-line Masters
The Complete ESL/EFL Cooperative and
  Communicative Activity Book
Easy Vocabulary Games
Vocabulary Games
Advanced Vocabulary Games
Play and Practice!
Basic Vocabulary Builder
Practical Vocabulary Builder
Beginning Activities for English
  Language Learners
Intermediate Activities for English
  Language Learners
Advanced Activities for English
  Language Learners

Language-Skills Texts
Starting English with a Smile
English with a Smile
More English with a Smile
English Survival Series
  Building Vocabulary, Recognizing Details,
  Identifying Main Ideas, Writing Sentences
  and Paragraphs, Using the Context
English Across the Curriculum
Essentials of Reading and Writing English
Everyday English
Everyday Situations for Communicating in
  English
Learning to Listen in English
Listening to Communicate in English
Communication Skillbooks
Living in the U.S.A.
Basic English Vocabulary Builder Activity Book
Basic Everyday Spelling Workbook
Practical Everyday Spelling Workbook

Advanced Readings and Communicative
  Activities for Oral Proficiency
Practical English Writing Skills
Express Yourself in Written English
Campus English
English Communication Skills for Professionals
Speak English!
Read English!
Write English!
Orientation in American English
Building English Sentences
Grammar for Use
Grammar Step-by-Step
Listening by Doing
Reading by Doing
Speaking by Doing
Vocabulary by Doing
Writing by Doing
Look, Think and Write

Life- and Work-Skills Texts
English for Success
Building Real Life English Skills
Everyday Consumer English
Book of Forms
Essential Life Skills series
Finding a Job in the United States
English for Adult Living
Living in English
Prevocational English

TOEFL and University Preparation
NTC's Preparation Course for the TOEFL®
NTC's Practice Tests for the TOEFL®
How to Apply to American Colleges
  and Universities
The International Student's Guide
  to the American University

Dictionaries and References
ABC's of Languages and Linguistics
Everyday American English Dictionary
Building Dictionary Skills in
  English (workbook)
Beginner's Dictionary of American
  English Usage
Beginner's English Dictionary
  Workbook
NTC's American Idioms Dictionary
NTC's Dictionary of American Slang
  and Colloquial Expressions
NTC's Dictionary of Phrasal Verbs
NTC's Dictionary of Grammar Terminology
Essential American Idioms
Contemporary American Slang
Forbidden American English
101 American English Idioms
101 American English Proverbs
Practical Idioms
Essentials of English Grammar
The Complete ESL/EFL Resource Book
Safari Grammar
Safari Punctuation
303 Dumb Spelling Mistakes
TESOL Professional Anthologies
  Grammar and Composition
  Listening, Speaking, and Reading
  Culture

For further information or a current catalog, write:
National Textbook Company
a division of *NTC Publishing Group*
4255 West Touhy Avenue
Lincolnwood, Illinois 60646-1975 U.S.A.

NTC